11 APR 2002

646.71

TIREE HIGH SCHOOL
LIBRARY

WISE *h* **GUIDES**

SPOTS

Anita Naik

Illustrated by Jennifer Graham
Consultant: Alison Dudley,
Acne Support Group

D0314337

Text copyright 2000 © Anita Naik
Illustrations copyright 2000 © Jennifer Graham
Published by Hodder Children's Books 2000

Design by Fiona Webb

The rights of Anita Naik and Jennifer Graham to be identified as the
author and illustrator of the work have been asserted by them in
accordance with the Copyright, Designs and Patents Act 1988.

10 9 8 7 6 5 4 3 2 1

ISBN: 0 340 75737 X

All rights reserved. No part of this publication may be reproduced,
stored in a retrieval system, or transmitted, in any form or by any
means, without the prior written permission of the publisher, nor be
otherwise circulated in any form of binding or cover other than that in
which it is published and without a similar condition being imposed on
the subsequent purchaser.

The information in this book has been thoroughly researched
and checked for accuracy. Neither the author nor the publisher
can accept any responsibility for any loss, injury or damage
incurred as a result of using this book.

Printed by The Guernsey Press Company Limited

Hodder Children's Books
a division of Hodder Headline
338 Euston Road
London NW1 3BH

Contents

Other essential

BULLYING
Michele Elliott

DIVORCE AND SEPARATION
Matthew Whyman

DRUGS
Anita Naik

EATING
Anita Naik

PERIODS
Charlotte Owen

SELF ESTEEM
Anita Naik

SEX
Anita Naik

SMOKING
Matthew Whyman

YOUR RIGHTS
Anita Naik

See page 96 for more details.

Introduction

When I was fourteen years old, every night before I went to bed I'd make a wish that I'd wake up with perfect, spot free skin. Unfortunately, most mornings I'd wake to find the opposite had happened and another huge volcano-like spot had appeared on my face. Of course, my spots were smaller than that, but after staring at them in the mirror for thirty minutes every morning, they always managed to grow to gigantic proportions in my mind.

When I wasn't looking forlornly into the bathroom mirror, I spent most of my spare time wandering the aisles of the local chemist, searching for amazing new spot products that I'd then have to persuade my mum to buy. I think over the years I tried everything, from a weird smelly face mask which required me to lie still for an hour, to a lotion that practically took my skin off, never mind zapping my zits. After failing on all those fronts

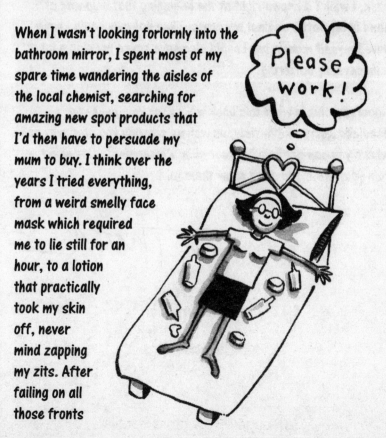

I followed the 'I know, I'll disguise it' method, which basically involved everything from caked on make-up in varying shades (which only made my spots look like spots with make-up on) to a plaster placed not too subtly over my biggest spot.

Finally, my sensible mum had enough of my whining and made me see the doctor, who promptly told me I had acne and gave me some orange tablets to take. I wasn't too pleased to know I had acne (even though I wasn't quite sure what it was) but I took the tablets and a year later I was clear of the pesky zits. Looking back, I wish I'd known right at the beginning that help was at hand in my battle against my spots. Then not only could I have saved myself money, but I could also have saved my skin a lot of unnecessary battering.

Hopefully, this is what this book will do for you: save you needless worry and anxiety, as well as showing you how, why and where you can get help for your skin. Remember, spots won't ruin your life if you don't allow them to.

Anita

CHAPTER ONE

What is skin?

"Skin is the stuff that stops your bones from popping out. It's like material which covers cushions. It helps protect you from getting hurt."

Lee, 10

"Skin is the stuff zits pop out of."

Becca, 12

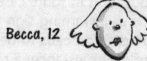

Believe it or not, your skin is your body's largest living, breathing organ. It is the super-strong protective, outer layer between your vital organs and the world of bacteria and pollution.

If you think about it, it's a remarkable organ. OK – now and again it lets you down with spots, scars and cuts, but you couldn't do without it.

Not only is it waterproof, it's also pretty good at repairing itself. Think about the last time you grazed your knee or cut yourself. It's likely your skin was ripped and you bled, and yet a week later the very same cut had probably healed without even a scar – unless you picked at the scab!

Better still, the skin is the body's extra-sensitive receptor. It knows when you're hot, so it releases sweat and lays the hairs on your body down so that air can cool your skin. And it knows when you're cold, so it covers you in goose bumps (which are in fact tiny muscles just under your skin contracting in response to coldness or fear). When you get goose bumps, the hairs or your arms and legs spring up into action and trap the heat leaving your body, to help keep you warmer.

Your skin also plays an important part in revealing a whole host of disorders and diseases that might be attacking your body, and in some cases it acts as a warning sign that something needs to be done. For instance, a rash might indicate an allergic reaction to something you've eaten or touched. Heat bumps are a sign you are overheating and need to cool down, and suntan is a sign the sun is damaging your skin.

YOU ARE ALLERGIC TO YOUR FACE CREAM

The skin's other tasks includes manufacturing the vitamin D it absorbs from sunlight into a nutrient which helps us get the best out of our food, especially calcium, which is important in strengthening our bones.

THE STRUCTURE OF THE SKIN

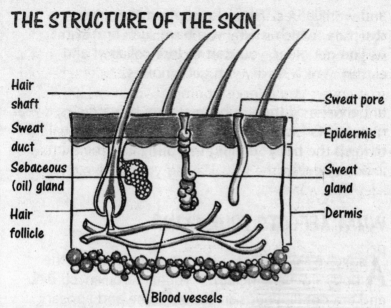

Hair shaft

Sweat duct

Sebaceous (oil) gland

Hair follicle

Sweat pore

Epidermis

Sweat gland

Dermis

Blood vessels

To understand how and why the skin changes, you first have to get down to the nitty gritty of how skin is made up.

Even though your skin looks pretty thin from the outside, it's actually made up of two complicated sheets.

The outer sheet is body tissue known as the epidermis. This tissue consists of billions of layers of cells (tiny structures invisible to the naked eye) which are hard, tough and strong.

The inner sheet is known as the dermis, and is more complicated than the epidermis. It is body tissue too, but this time it's a stringy kind. This tissue is mixed with two very important substances called elastin and collagen which are responsible for keeping skin plump and wrinkle free. They also support the skin's structure, which is why you have such firm skin. As you get older, you start to lose collagen and elastin, which is why you get wrinkles.

In between all these substances are hair follicles, sweat glands and blood vessels, all performing essential jobs to keep the body running smoothly and the skin looking healthy.

WHAT AFFECTS YOUR SKIN?

As we've said, the skin is a good indicator of the body's general health. If you eat a balanced diet and are not ill, your skin should shine and appear healthy. If you've been ill for a long time or off your food, your skin may look dull and perhaps even grey. This is because you are run down and, like the rest of your body's organs, your skin has no energy to look healthy.

Health aside, the cold and heat will also change the way your skin looks, especially if you don't take care to protect it in harsh or very hot weather. You may not realise that there are two other important factors which affect the way your skin looks: your emotions and your hormones. Before you hit puberty, your hormones will not affect your skin because there won't be such high levels of them racing around your body. However, you may find that your emotions already affect the way your skin looks. Perhaps you blush when you're happy or embarrassed, or go very pale when you are scared or frightened. These are very natural responses and happen in adults as well as young people.

FIVE COMMON SKIN CONDITIONS

Blushing

> "My friends tease me because I go red every time a boy speaks to me or a teacher asks me a question in class. Why does this happen? It's really embarrassing."
>
> Helen, 13

As your skin is a living, breathing organ, it responds to both emotional and physical sensations. Blushing happens when you are embarrassed, pleased or shy. Your body heats up, and this causes the blood vessels in the dermis (inner layer of skin) to dilate or get bigger. This in turn makes the skin look a pinkish red colour, hence the blush. Some people blush more than others.

Bruising

> "How come the skin changes colour when you fall on it? I got some fantastic bruises when I fell off my bike which went lots of different colours, but I don't know why that happened."
>
> Tom, 12

Bruises occur when there is a trauma to the skin. When this happens, blood in the skin doesn't flow through it as normal but forms into small blood clots.

These clots then turn black or a bluish purple colour and show through the skin as a bruise. Bruises can go all sorts of marvellous yellowy green colours as the skin heals.

Freckles

"What are freckles? I've got loads of them all over my face and arms but my sister hasn't got any. They never go away, not even in the winter."

Fiona, 12

Freckles look like little faint marks on the skin. They are actually small flat spots of skin pigment, sometimes known as summer kisses because they increase naturally with sunlight.

Stretch Marks

"When my brother grew last year, he was left with funny little marks a bit like silvery wrinkles on the skin across his back. What are these?"

Ann, 14

Stretch marks are breakdowns in the elastic fibres of the skin. They usually occur when the skin has been stretched excessively, like during pregnancy, teenage growth spurts or when you put on weight quickly. There is no miracle cure for these red, purple or silvery white marks, but as you grow up, it is likely that these will fade in time.

Moles

"My mum has a black mark on her skin and she says it's a mole. I don't have any of these, but my brother has them all over his back. What are they, and do you need to see a doctor about them?"

James, 12

A mole (sometimes known as a beauty spot) looks like a dark dot on the skin. It is usually much darker than normal skin colour, and often appears to be black and slightly raised. It's nothing more than a small collection of different skin pigment cells gathered together in one place. Some moles are tiny, others are bigger. You only need to see a doctor if the mole is sore or suddenly starts to grow.

FIVE COMMON SKIN COMPLAINTS YOU CAN DO SOMETHING ABOUT

Warts

These are small cauliflower-like lumps that appear on the skin, usually the face or fingers, and are caused by Human Papilloma virus (HPV). They need to be treated by a doctor.

Cold Sores

These are small blister-like sores, usually found around the corners of your mouth. They are the result of the Herpes Simplex virus, and occur when you have been stressed, unwell or in strong sunlight. Again, these need to be treated by a doctor as they can be contagious.

Rashes

A rash might look like tiny red sore spots and will often spread over a small area and be itchy. Rashes are not zits but a sign your skin is inflamed, either by an illness or an allergic reaction to something. This can be anything from sunlight or something you've eaten, to soap and face cream. Your doctor will be able to help.

Abscesses

An abscess looks like a sore reddish-yellow hard lump and is actually a bubble of pus inside a hair follicle or sweat gland due to an infection caused by bacteria. You should go and see your doctor if you have an abscess.

Lumps and Cysts

Unlike an abscess, a cyst doesn't look sore, though it does appear like a smallish bubble on the skin (sometimes the size of a pea, other times several centimetres in diameter), and might be fairly hard. The hardness is caused by fluid build-up in a sebaceous gland. Again, go and see your doctor who will be able to treat any lumps or cysts.

HOW SKIN RENEWS ITSELF

"My pet snake has to shed its whole skin when it grows, but we don't have to do this. How does our skin grow?"

Lee, 12

B elieve it or not, your skin actually renews itself every two to three weeks (although this renewal time lengthens as you age). So your skin is always changing, as it frequently replaces the cells which make up your epidermis. This renewal happens quite naturally as old cells drop off at the rate of about five per cent a day and are immediately replaced by new, younger cells. Most of us don't notice this as it happens so gently and easily. Interestingly enough, dead skin cells apparently make up 90% of all household dust.

SKIN COLOUR

"I know why my skin is dark, but how come my friend has a different colour to me, when our parents come from the same place?"

Sheena, 13

Ever wondered how skin colour comes about, and why we all have different shades of colour? Well, this occurs because something called melanin, also known as skin pigment or colour, is working behind the scenes. The job of the melanin is to protect the skin from the sun's harmful ultraviolet rays, and it makes the skin naturally go darker. People whose families originally came from hotter and sunnier climates are born with darker skin, which contains lots of melanin to protect them from the sun's harmful rays.

HOW AND WHY SKIN AGES

"My mum's skin has suddenly become very dry and
wrinkly. I don't know why this has happened. Is she
doing something wrong?"

Tina, 14

Skin ages because the special fibres it contains,
collagen and elastin, start running out as we get
older. The moistness and lubrication of our skin also
changes, and skin becomes dryer and more fragile.
This means the firmness we have as children and
young adults gives way to saggy, droopy skin with
wrinkles.

But age is not the only factor behind changing skin.
The breakdown in the skin's fibres also happens if you
blast yourself with strong sunlight, smoke or drink too
much alcohol. If you think you're too young to worry
about such skin damage, consider this: the majority
of sun damage to your skin occurs *before* you're
eighteen years old!

PERFECT SKIN

"I love the way models look in magazines and am
desperate to get skin like theirs. How can I get my
skin to look perfect? No matter what I do it still
looks lumpy and never clear like in those pictures."

Debbie, 14

If you believe everything you see and read, you might think 100% flawless skin exists, if only you could afford to buy enough skin products. This is not true: perfect skin does not exist. All the images of perfection you see in magazines are just illusions.

Think of the close-up of a model's face on a magazine cover or in an advert. It looks amazingly perfect, doesn't it? Well, it is, but not because the model has spent hundreds of pounds on skin-care.

BEFORE

AFTER

Despite the make-up, good lighting and professional photography, something else is at work here. This something else is called airbrushing or touching up. This is done on computer and means that a photograph of even the most blemished face can be zapped clear, evenly colour-toned and de-wrinkled in a matter of minutes – making the picture of the model look totally perfect.

THE SECRET OF GOOD SKIN

"I would love to have clear, fantastic looking skin. Is there a secret to having great skin with no spots? My mum says there isn't, but there must be because I see loads of people like this."

Joy, 13

Of course, some people do have naturally good skin (not perfect, but good), just as some people have good hair, good figures or good teeth. However, this is usually because of something called an hereditary trait or gene. This is a message passed on to your body by your parents' bodies when you were conceived, before you were even born. So if you want to see what your chances are of having good skin for life or of being acne-free through your teens, check with your parents on how they fared.

If your parents had problematic skin, don't worry: there are still many things you can do to help your skin look the very best that it can. Even better, these things don't involve wearing expensive creams, having facials or cosmetic surgery.

10 WAYS TO MAKE THE MOST OF YOUR SKIN

1 Read the rest of this book.
2 Try to take on as much of it as you can.
3 Don't be a couch potato: do some exercise and take care of your skin.
4 Wash your face every day.
5 Girls, take your make-up off every day and boys, learn to shave correctly.
6 Get enough sleep.
7 Wear sun protection.
8 Drink plenty of water.
9 Don't smoke.
10 Don't drink too much alcohol.

DID YOU KNOW...

- Over your entire life span you will lose about 35 lbs of dead skin cells.
- The hardest and thickest skin is on the soles of your feet.
- The thinnest skin is over your eyes and on your lips.
- Facial skin is about 0.12 mm thick.
- Collagen implants are used in cosmetic surgery to pump up lips.
- Implanted collagen used to come from cows, or the red parts of a rooster's head. Now it is usually synthetic.
- Nails and hair are extensions of the skin, made up of a substance called keratin.
- The skin on the whole of an adult body weighs approximately 4 kg.
- 1 square inch of skin contains: 4.5 m of blood vessels, 650 sweat glands and 100 oil glands.
- Women in the UK spend £5 million a year on skin-care products.

CHAPTER TWO

What factors affect your skin?

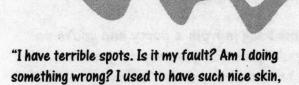

"I have terrible spots. Is it my fault? Am I doing something wrong? I used to have such nice skin, but now it's all covered in zits and blackheads. It's really depressing."

Amy, 14

As we've already pointed out, there are many things that stand between good and not-so-good skin. In this chapter we show you some of the factors that will affect your skin and change it as you get older – factors, which as you'll see in later chapters, directly affect spots and acne.

The good news is, there are lots of things you can do to make the most of your skin. Read on and you'll find out why teenage skin is prone to zits and blackheads, and exactly what you can do to help your skin look and feel good.

● QUIZ ●

ARE YOU YOUR SKIN'S WORST ENEMY?

How much do you know about helping your skin to stay relatively spot free and healthy? Do you do all you can for it, or are you your skin's own worst enemy? Test yourself with this quiz and find out how much you really know!

1 **You come back in from a party and you're so tired you're practically asleep on your feet. What's the most important thing you should do for your skin at night?**
   a) *Wash your face or take off your make-up*
   b) *Get eight hours sleep*
   c) *Drink two glasses of water*

2 **You want a tan. What's the best way to do it?**
   a) *Go on a sun bed*
   b) *Sit in the sun*
   c) *Try a fake tan*

3 **Acne is the result of...**
   a) *Eating chips*
   b) *Your body changing at puberty*
   c) *An allergy*

4 **Boys are more likely to have bad skin than girls because...**
   a) They are less likely to wash properly
   b) They have to shave
   c) They have different levels of hormones

5 **There's only one way to treat acne and spots.**
   a) True
   b) False
   c) You can't treat them

6 **If your parents had acne, then will you have it too?**
   a) No
   b) Not necessarily
   c) Yes

7 **What kind of face cream is best for your skin?**
   a) An anti-bacterial cream
   b) One that doesn't block your pores
   c) You should never use cream on teenage skin

8 **What does skin type mean?**
   a) Nothing, it's a load of old nonsense
   b) It's just a way to make sure you use the right products for your skin
   c) It means whether you have spots or not

9 Most adults don't get spots because...
   a) They've grown out of them
   b) They know how to eat properly
   c) They know how to hide them

10 Who can give you the best advice about your skin?
   a) Someone on a make-up counter
   b) Your mum
   c) Your GP

ANSWERS

1	A	2	C	3	B
4	C	5	B	6	B
7	B	8	B	9	A
10	C				

How did you score? Under 3 correct answers: you need to read this book twice! 3–6: you're on the right track, but you might need a few more tips. 7–10: you're a skin guru all right, but carry on reading – you might discover something new.

HORMONES AND PUBERTY

Yes, it's the dreaded 'P' word again: puberty. The time of your life when body chemicals known as hormones literally affect everything about you, from your height right down to your shoe size. Well, not surprisingly, puberty also affects the way your skin looks.

Puberty in Girls

While puberty happens to everyone, it rarely happens at the same time for anyone. Puberty occurs because of chemicals in our bodies called hormones. These hormones regulate our physical growth and produce the changes in our height and weight. Our hormones are released from small organs around our body called endocrine glands. Once released, these hormones travel around via the bloodstream and start to make changes to our bodies.

The most important female sex hormone is oestrogen, and this is produced by the ovaries. It is this hormone which gradually stimulates the development of breasts, initiates your periods, changes your moods and affects your skin. Oestrogen is also a very important skin regulator. A good supply means your skin will look supple, soft and healthy. This is why girls usually have better skin than boys (women have much more oestrogen than men, who only have tiny amounts). However, girls also have small amounts of the male hormone known as testosterone. This is the hormone which triggers acne and causes spots (see Chapter Four, page 49).

Unfortunately, you also have to contend with periods at puberty and one of the side-effects of periods can often be spots. This is because the female period (also known as the menstrual cycle) is controlled by your hormones, especially the two female hormones, oestrogen and progestogen. Both hormones increase and decrease rapidly during the different stages of your cycle, which is why you might find yourself going through many varied emotions before your period arrives each month.

Prior to your period arriving you might also find yourself craving sweet things, especially chocolate, and you might also find that your skin breaks out in

spots. Contrary to popular belief, these spots do not occur because you have eaten chocolate but because your hormones are affecting your skin, causing more blocked pores and therefore causing spots to appear.

Throughout the whole of puberty your hormones will be doing things like this to your skin, which is why teenage skin can be so problematic. Of course, not everyone will have skin problems during puberty, but it's perfectly normal to start getting spots at this time.

Puberty in Boys

The male physical and emotional transformation of puberty usually occurs about two years later than in girls. Like puberty in girls, it occurs because of chemicals called hormones. Again, it is the sex hormone testosterone which is behind the body and skin changes. This hormone encourages growth and causes the sexual changes in your body.

At puberty these hormones also activate certain glands to produce more oil to lubricate both your skin and your hair. You'll find that your skin starts to become coarser, you'll develop facial hair and you'll probably get spots. This happens because the ducts that take the excess oil to the surface of your skin and the follicles that take facial hair to the surface become blocked, and infected swellings occur, leading to acne. Also, with acne, dead skin cells get sticky and can't be shed very quickly. This helps to cause a blockage where the excess oil gets trapped, and bacteria starts to form the 'spot'.

FOOD AND YOUR SKIN

 "I know chocolate and chips don't cause spots, but are there any types of food that can give me better skin?"

Sue, 14

Some dermatologists (skin doctors) pooh-pooh the idea that there might be any link between diet and skin, but nutritionists (food, vitamin and nutrient specialists) will tell you that a diet rich in fresh vegetables, fruit and carbohydrates will benefit your skin. They believe this is because healthy skin is dependent on a healthy kidney and liver, which work better with a balanced diet. If your system has to use its energy in breaking down lots of junk food and sugar, the kidneys and liver can't work as well, which in turn leads to a build up of waste in the body. However, many dermatologists believe this theory is untrue and that the only reason a good diet helps you to maintain healthy skin is because certain vitamins, such as vitamin C which is found in fresh fruit and vegetables, help the skin to fight infection.

Essential vitamins for skin health

Vitamins	Source	Role
A	Carrots, meat and dairy produce	Production of skin cells.
B1	Cereals, Marmite	Repairs skin.
C	Citrus fruits	Keeps skin looking healthy and fights infection.
D	Eggs, fish, liver and also from the sun (always protect your skin with SPF cream)	Builds strong bones and skin.
E	Nuts, vegetables and eggs	Anti-oxidant (helps fight against ageing). Very good in cream form, may help reduce scar tissue.
Zinc	Dairy products and meat	Repairs wounds.

The importance of a healthy diet

According to a Health Education Authority survey, 34% of young adults think that healthy foods are 'too boring'. But eating healthily doesn't have to mean saying no to foods you like and choosing fruit instead. Healthy eating is for everyone and is about making sure you have a well-balanced diet with plenty of the following:

- Carbohydrates (bread, pasta, potatoes, rice)
- Vegetables
- Fruit
- Dairy products (butter, milk, cheese, yoghurt)
- Cereals
- Fish
- Lean meat
- Eggs

You should only have these in moderation:
- Fizzy drinks
- Chocolate
- Sweets
- Biscuits
- Cakes
- Crisps

And drink lots and lots of water –
at least eight glasses or one litre
a day. Not only does this detoxify
your system, getting rid of waste,
but it will also stop you becoming
dehydrated.

EXERCISE AND YOUR SKIN

Nothing is better for you than regular exercise.
Studies show that just twenty minutes of aerobic
exercise three times a week increases your fitness.
It also decreases stress, helps keep depression away,
prevents sleeplessness and increases your all-round
energy. Better still, it helps to keep your skin glowing
with vitality.

This is because when you exercise, oxygen flows to every area of your body, helping to regenerate cells and kick-starting your digestive system. While not all exercise gives you the same kind of fitness, strength (muscular endurance like working with weights), flexibility (stretching and body conditioning) and aerobic exercise (burns fat and builds up the heart, lung and circulation capacity) can all be achieved through simple things like swimming, and walking regularly. The most important type of exercise for health and your skin is aerobic exercise.

Exercise tips

- For all-round fitness, do a mixture of activities that work your muscles, improve flexibility and increase aerobic capacity.
- Roller-skating is brilliant for aerobic fitness, strength and flexibility.
- Dancing is also good for all of the above.
- Climbing the stairs for twenty minutes at a time is good aerobic exercise.
- If you are interested in a particular sport and don't know how to get involved, contact the Sports Council (telephone: 020 7273 1500).

THE SUN AND YOUR SKIN

"Some people say you shouldn't lie in the sun because it's bad for your skin, but some people say you should if you're spotty because it really helps to get rid of acne. Is this true?"

Tina, 14

The sun can make acne *look* better, but only in the very short term. If you sit in the sun to zap your spots, you risk doing far greater long-term damage to your skin. For starters, apart from putting yourself at risk from skin cancer, you'll also end up with ageing, saggy, baggy and wrinkle-filled skin. So unless you want to apply for a free bus pass by the time you're thirty, stay out of the sun and use sun protection cream with a high sun protection factor (SPF) – nothing under SPF 15. Also make sure your cream protects against UVB rays (which burn your skin) and UVA rays (which age your skin).

Why all the fuss? Well, basically, the sun is the number one enemy of skin. If you go on holiday to any hot country, you'll notice how the local people know this already (sadly, most people in the UK don't). Locals know you can't lie out in the midday sun, even with protective sun cream on. They know that fair skin burns more easily and that the sun ages and wrinkles skin. They know to wear a hat when they are walking around. Most importantly, they know that people who aren't used to the sun should build up the time they spend in it and not throw themselves into the heat for eight hours on the first day of their holidays!

Protecting your skin in the sun

- Wear the right sun protection cream. Studies now show that in very hot sunlight, anything below SPF 15 offers no protection.
- Make sure your sunscreen protects you from UVA and UVB rays.
- Don't put oil or normal cream on your skin when you're going into the sun – you will burn yourself.
- If you are very fair, wear a total sun block.
- The safest sunscreen for people who are fair or who have ever burnt themselves is sun cream with a high factor, above SPF 15.
- If you are fair-skinned you will not tan, no matter how long you stay in the sun.
- Keep to the shade: sudden sharp bursts of intense sunlight is very dangerous to the skin.
- Don't sit out at midday. Stay inside from eleven to three o'clock.
- Protect your head by wearing a hat.
- Be careful in the water or on the sand. Both reflect and intensify sunlight on your skin.
- Sunbeds produce mainly UVA rays, which are less dangerous than natural light; but they will damage your skin if used regularly.

- If you do get severe sunburn, see your doctor.
- Remember, even on non-sunny days you can get burnt by UVB rays, so *always* use a sunscreen when you're outside.
- 90% OF SUN DAMAGE TO THE SKIN IS DONE BY THE TIME A PERSON IS EIGHTEEN YEARS OLD.

SLEEP AND YOUR SKIN

"How much sleep is a person supposed to have? I seem to only need six hours but my mum doesn't believe me. She says eight hours is what everyone needs to look healthy."

Allie, 14

There's a lot to be said for the phrase 'getting your beauty sleep'. The fact is, there's nothing quite so important to the skin (except perhaps water) than sleeping. This is because the primary purpose of sleep is to let your body recoup its energies and renew itself.

Sleep does a number of wonderful things to the skin. For starters, skin cells regenerate as you sleep. Studies show that the cell division which restores our cells increases by 250% when we sleep. This doesn't happen when we're awake because our energy is needed elsewhere.

SMOKING AND YOUR SKIN

"I wouldn't really call myself a smoker. I smoke much less than some of my mates – I only have about three cigarettes a day. Surely this isn't going to ruin my skin?"

Fiona, 15

When you smoke, the following things happen: your heart speeds up, your blood pressure increases and you suddenly feel more alert. However, as you become addicted to the nicotine in cigarettes, you will feel jittery, irritable and depressed. The smoke you've inhaled will circulate round your body, destroying your circulatory system and coating your lungs with tar.

Maybe you've just started smoking or you only have the odd one or two, so you might think this won't hold true for you. Or you may think the health risks associated with smoking have very little to do with how you look on the outside. WRONG!

Smoking destroys your skin in the following ways:

Smoking gives you wrinkles

Studies show smokers have far more wrinkles than non-smokers, and they develop them at a much earlier age. This is because smoking damages the collagen and elastin fibres in the skin, making it lose its firmness.

The actual process of smoking a cigarette makes you more prone to wrinkles around your lips, eyes and nose.

Smoking gives you broken facial veins

Smoking also destroys your body's circulation. This means the veins that carry the blood round your body are more fragile, and smokers can often been seen with small broken red veins on their face.

Smoking gives you 'grey' skin

Healthy skin looks healthy in the way you'd expect it to: it glows and looks fresh. Smokers' skins have a different look, thanks to bad circulation and the breakdown in skin fibres. Smoking also stops the absorption of vitamin C, which is essential for healthy skin.

Five tips on how to stop smoking

- Decide to give up and give yourself a deadline for your last cigarette.
- Imagine what you'll do with all the money you'll save by not smoking.
- Ask your friends and family to support you.
- Keep away from situations you know you'll feel tempted to smoke in.
- Read *Wise Guides: Smoking* (see page 103).

STRESS AND YOUR SKIN

"Why do I always get a spot when I'm about to go somewhere good like a party? It almost seems like spots somehow know when I'm getting excited about going out and they pop up just to ruin my evening."

Ellie, 12

Stress is said to be another major factor in producing dried out and sometimes spotty skin. If you're at all unsure about this, think about the last time you had an exam or were about to go on a hot date (funny how a spot always appears just as you need to look 'perfect', isn't it?). Well, if this sounds like you, you can blame your stress hormones. The second you feel anxious and worried, these hormones are released and flood through your body. Although it's practically impossible to live a stress-free life, you can help yourself by doing some or all of the following:

- Give yourself a break. No one is going to think you're unattractive just because you have a spot.
- Don't make yourself overly anxious about an event like a date, which is meant to be a pleasure, not a duty.
- It's easy to eat and sleep badly when you feel stressed, but both increase the chances of your skin breaking out in spots.
- Talk about how you feel to someone you trust.

PERSPIRATION AND YOUR SKIN

Sweating is a normal bodily function. It is the body's natural cooling down system and regulates body temperature. Perspiration under the arms is normal, but during puberty and around our periods our sweat glands can over-produce and may cause excessive sweating. This can lead to a clogging of pores, and spots in areas where the skin can't breathe.

Help yourself by wearing cotton clothes that allow your skin to breathe. Also, wash at least once a day, and use an anti-perspirant which will help control your perspiration, rather than just a deodorant, which only masks it.

TIPS FOR HEALTHY SKIN

- Drink lots of water: it stops your skin dehydrating. Remember, no matter how much water we apply to the outside of the skin, the majority is needed on the inside. Up to 90% of the water our bodies use is absorbed from our food and drink via the colon (the large intestine). For healthy skin, it is recommended that we drink at least one litre of water a day.
- Don't smoke: it robs your skin of oxygen and dehydrates your skin.
- Laugh a lot! Children laugh and smile on average 400 times a day, an adult only 15 times. Laughter is good for you as it speeds up your heart and boosts your circulation and oxygen intake. It also leaves your nerves and muscles relaxed.

- Go out into the fresh air, and get your circulation going by doing some exercise.
- Eat lots of fruit and vegetables.
- Relax more.
- Make sure you always take your make-up off.

● CHAPTER THREE ●

What is problem skin?

"It's skin that looks spotty and greasy, where you've got more spots than clear skin. My brother's fourteen and I think he's got problem skin."

Sue, 12

"Problem skin is skin that is dry and wrinkly and flakes off, like dandruff. It's usually old people who get problem skin and they have to spend loads of money on face creams. You're really unlucky if you get it when you're young."

Jack, 11

"It's just normal skin. People selling cosmetics call it 'problem' skin so you'll spend more money on their products."

Lisa, 14

If you've ever wandered around a make-up counter in a department store, you'll have noticed how there are millions of products promising you perfect skin and/or showing you how you can obtain perfect skin. If you've been unlucky enough to be accosted by

a skin-care specialist in one of these stores
(i.e. someone working on a make-up counter),
you'll probably have been given lots of 'advice' on
how to 'help' your skin. Usually, this means someone
identifying your 'problem' skin type and then involves
you handing over your life savings for a 'special'
cream to save your skin.

Don't be fooled by this 'problem skin' jargon – all
skin, like all hair, is divided into particular groups, and
none are problematic in a major way because all the
problems can be dealt with.

Skin is basically divided into five groups:

- Normal
- Combination (dry and oily)
- Oily
- Dry
- Sensitive

Remember, these classifications don't mean your skin is 'bad', they just indicate the kind of skin you have thanks to your biology, your genetics and your lifestyle. You can learn to make the most of your skin by identifying your skin type, but don't fool yourself into thinking your skin type is some kind of 'bad' thing you have to work on.

KNOW YOUR SKIN TYPE

How to identify normal skin

Normal skin isn't skin that looks completely perfect all the time, or skin that never ever gets spots. Normal skin is just skin that isn't either particularly dry or oily. Basically, if you don't have many problems with your skin and if it doesn't match one of the other categories, it's probably normal.

You can look after normal skin in the following ways:

- Wash your face gently twice a day (see page 44 for a guide to washing your face).
- Use an inexpensive moisturiser.

How to identify combination skin

Combination skin isn't skin that's dripping with oil in one place and peeling off in others.

Combination skin is dry, flaky cheeks and an oily T-zone going from your forehead down your nose to your chin. When we say oily, we don't mean literally dripping with oil, but shiny and sweaty-looking skin. The best way to test this is to pat your face with a tissue, and see if the tissue absorbs anything.

This type of skin is prone to blemishes on the T-zone and not on the cheeks.

You can look after combination skin in the following ways:

- Don't use soap as this dries out the skin even more. If you do use a soap, make sure it is a pH balanced one as this is closest to the skin's natural acidity levels. Or try a soap-free cleanser.
- Use an inexpensive oil-free moisturiser on your cheeks, and apply only light bits to your T-zone. Too much moisturiser on the T-zone may make your skin more oily.
- Don't scrub your skin hard as this only makes the sebaceous glands (oil producing glands) work harder. Gentle but frequent exfoliation using something like oatmeal – yes, plain oatmeal from the supermarket or health food shop! – may help to 'buff' the skin.
- Remember, if your skin is sore or broken, do not exfoliate.

How to identify oily skin

Oily skin isn't skin literally dripping with oil and moisture. Oily skin is skin with large pores that looks shiny even when it's not hot. If you're not sure if your skin is oily, try the tissue test. Gently place a tissue over your face and press down. Lift it off, and if the tissue is marked with moisture you have oily skin.

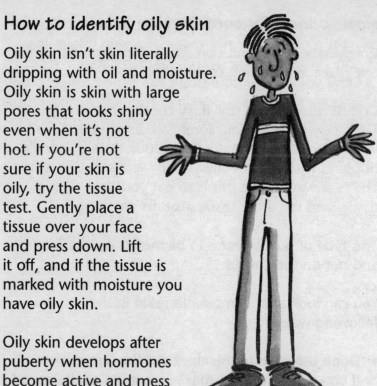

Oily skin develops after puberty when hormones become active and mess up sebum production (oil production in the skin). This makes your skin look greasy and sweaty. It also makes you prone to spots as the sebum blocks up the skin pores and causes infections. Before you think you've got the worst deal, consider this – people with oily skin rarely get wrinkles, because their skin never dries out. So while you might have to deal with teenage spots, you're unlikely to look wrinkly.

You can look after oily skin in the following ways:

- Don't over-wash your face. This will not get rid of the oil, but just increase production of the oil glands.

- Use a skin toner to remove excess cleanser. The right toner should not make your skin tingle, feel sore or tight. If any of these things happen, it's likely your skin products are too strong for your skin and are stripping your skin of moisture. This in turn may cause more sebum production as the skin tries to add moisture. Contrary to popular belief, toner does not close pores (nothing can do this).
- Use light face lotions (creams that are runny, not solid, when poured).
- Seek help from your GP if your spots are getting you down or aren't improving (see Chapter 5, page 76).

How to identify dry skin

Dry skin isn't skin which peels off in layers.

Dry skin is skin which tends to look red in patches and can even be flaky. Sometimes, the skin will look chapped and peeling. If this looks like your skin, it's definitely dry skin.

The good news is that this type of skin rarely gets spots because there is little oil production going on. For this reason, this type of skin is associated with older people, who have a slower hormone production rate. The bad news is that this type of skin is prone to wrinkles and can be itchy at times.

You can look after dry skin in the following ways:

- Use a moisturiser and make sure it's rich enough for your skin.

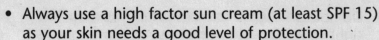

- Always use a high factor sun cream (at least SPF 15) as your skin needs a good level of protection.
- Don't use alcohol based toners and cleansers: these strip the skin of even more moisture and make it even drier.
- Don't use soaps which leave your skin feeling tight.

How to identify sensitive skin

Sensitive skin isn't skin that gets red and lumpy every time you put something on it.

Sensitive skin is skin which can be blotchy, sometimes itchy and can react quickly to certain soaps, or extremes in temperature. This type of skin is very similar to dry skin, except that it reacts strongly to certain things placed on it, like certain brands of make-up, creams, sun creams and soaps. If you put something on your face and your skin feels itchy, or it develops a rash or tiny red spots, it's likely you are having an allergic reaction to something.

You can look after sensitive skin in the following ways:

- Use hypo-allergenic, unperfumed products (perfumed products often irritate sensitive skins).
- Use the less rule: less time spent on your face and less products used.
- Always patch-test products for 24 hours before you apply something all over – this means you should use the product on a very small part of your skin and see if it reacts within 24 hours. If not, go ahead and use the product all over. If it does react, then don't use the product.

- Do not use alcohol based products as these are very drying.
- Don't go for expensive products: often the cheapest and simplest ones work best.
- 'Natural' doesn't mean it won't affect your skin. You can be allergic to natural products as well.
- Seek help from your GP if your skin worsens and you don't know why.

Skin type tips

- Even if you're a boy, you need to clean and protect your skin if you want it to look good.
- Don't be fooled by expensive products as they are not always better than cheaper ones.
- Anti-ageing products are not necessary for young people – a moisturiser with SPF 15 is enough.
- You are the best judge of what's right for your skin. If something feels strange and tingly, it's probably not right for your skin type.
- Just because something works well for your best friend's skin doesn't mean it will work for you.
- Don't be afraid to seek help from your GP if your skin is irritating you. You could have any one of a number of skin complaints that can be easily treated.

WASHING YOUR FACE

So now you know what skin type you are, how should you look after your face? With so much contradictory beauty advice around, it can be hard to know what the right thing to do is. So here's a quick guide to washing dos and don'ts.

Soap and Facial Washes

Soap gets a lot of bad press. Ask around and you'll probably hear loads of people saying it's bad for your skin, it dries it out, it causes spots. However, soap has many things going for it. For starters, it's cheap and effective. What's more, as long as you use the right type of soap you should be fine – always use a soap with a pH balance of 5.5.

If you have oily skin, glycerine soaps (clear-looking soaps) are recommended. For sensitive and dry skins, use hypo-allergenic soaps (the label will tell you if a product is hypo-allergenic). And for combination skins, use soap-free soaps.

If you do wash with soap and your skin reacts badly or feels tight and uncomfortable, then try using something else. Facial washes are usually a better option because they are detergent-based rather than soap-based. If you use a facial wash, only use a small bit and always rinse your face well.

Facial Scrubs

These usually come in a tube and have some kind of exfoliant within them (granules designed to slough off dead skin cells). These scrubs are not meant for everyday use and there is much debate on whether or not they are needed. Basically, they work as a rough cleanser, designed to make your skin soft and shiny.

Some skin experts believe the skin-shedding cycle is efficient enough to rid itself of dead skin cells, without using a facial scrub. What's more, they feel that scrubs can rob the skin of moisture and scratch its surface (so you must always make sure the exfoliant isn't too harsh – if it scratches your hand, it will scratch your face). Other experts disagree and feel it can help skin to look healthier. Whatever you decide, never use exfoliants on spots or sensitive skin. And if your skin is oily, keep a careful look out to make sure the exfoliation doesn't make the skin oilier by activating the sebaceous glands.

Cleansing Creams and Lotions

These are designed to clean your face without washing it, so they are ideal for dry and sensitive skins. You apply them to your face and then wipe them off with either a tissue or cotton wool. Most lotions are a mixture of oil, water and cleanser and work by dissolving grime.

Moisturisers

Moisturisers are face creams designed to help protect moisture from being lost from the skin. They do this by acting as a barrier on the surface of the skin. Don't be fooled into thinking that face creams add moisture to the skin. This can only be done from the inside of your skin: moisture cannot be absorbed into the skin from the outside.

Always remember to use a moisturiser which:

- Suits your skin type.
- Contains SPF 15.
- Is non-comedogenic (won't block your pores).
- Is hypo-allergenic (tested to make sure it won't cause an allergy).
- Is cheap, because price has relatively little to do with how good a moisturiser is.

How to wash your face

While you might think this sounds ridiculous, it's important to know how to wash your skin properly. This means more than dunking your head in cold water, rubbing on a bit of soap and roughly towel-drying your skin.

1 Wash your face twice a day. As boring and time-consuming as this sounds, it will lessen the build-up of grime and help your skin to look better.
2 Use the right cleanser (see page 43) for your skin type, and apply it in small amounts. Rub gently – remember, the skin on your face is thin and delicate and years of treating it roughly will eventually show. Always remove your cleanser with damp cotton wool or a clean face-cloth.

3 Don't scrub at any spots, as this will only take off the top layer of skin, making your spots more prone to infection and causing redness and scars.

4 When you have washed off the cleanser with fresh water, pat your face dry with a towel. If you rub at your face you will irritate the skin, especially if it's dry already.

BIG PROBLEMS FOR SKIN

If you want to look after your skin, it's no good buying expensive face products, exercising and eating well if you're going to sabotage all the good work you're doing in the following ways:

1. SITTING IN THE SUN

"Is the sun really that bad? I know people are always saying to cover up or wear a sunblock, but surely sunbathing doesn't do that much harm."

Tina, 13

Sun tanning is the single most damaging thing you can do to your skin. Not only does it do permanent damage but it also ages the skin, makes acne worse in the long run and leads to skin cancer.

2. SMOKING

"Is it true that smoking makes your skin wrinkly, or is it just one of those scare stories your parents and teachers tell you to scare people off cigarettes?"

Sara, 12

We all know that smoking is bad for the health, causes cancer, and can kill you. But (as if that isn't enough), do you know what it can do to your skin, especially if you're under eighteen? Well, for a start, cigarettes contain over 4000 chemicals – this means that every time you take a puff, you are inhaling a whole load of nasties. Nasties which exit your body through your skin. This in turn means that smoking damages the collagen and elastin fibres of your skin. It makes your skin less firm and healthy looking, and adds deep premature lines (for more information see Chapter 2, pages 29–30).

3. NOT WASHING

"I never wash my face because I've heard it dries out the skin and causes more spots."

Julie, 13

While this sounds ridiculous, you'd be surprised at how many people remember to wash their hands and have a shower every day, but don't wash their face. Even if you're the healthiest person alive, there are still a number of environmental factors that will wreak havoc on your face, especially if you don't keep it clean. For starters, car exhaust fumes, other people's smoke, central heating and pollution all help to break down skin cells. This is because they are full of contaminants that take away moisture form the skin and block pores. You need to make sure you regularly clean your face, drink lots of water and take exercise; all these things will help your skin flush out the grime that can lead to blemishes and problem skin.

4. DIETING

"My mum says that dieting is very bad for you. She says that apart from not being a good way to keep slim, it ruins your skin and causes spots. Is this true?"

Lou, 14

Dieting, as well as being bad for your body, is pretty bad for your skin too. This is because for healthy, strong skin, girls need plenty of the female hormone, oestrogen. Your body needs body fat levels of roughly between 18–28% in order to produce it. Before you hit puberty, your body only carries 12% of body fat but at puberty this changes and levels rise to around 18–28% to help your body cope with the changes taking place.

Most people think of the word 'fat' and immediately feel negative, because these days it's drummed into us that fat is a bad thing we have to try and avoid. It's silly really, because fat is essential to the human body. We all need it to maintain and sustain our lives.

In fact, body fat is just stored energy. Its roles include cushioning our organs from damage, stopping us from feeling the cold, and most importantly, supplying our body with the energy and fuel it needs to do everyday things, from walking to talking.

If you diet and skip meals, your body's oestrogen production will slow down, and your skin will immediately be affected for the worse.

5. DRINKING ALCOHOL

"I've heard that drinking alcohol is supposed to be bad for the skin. What will it do to my face?"

Tom, 14

Do you fancy having blotchy dry skin, or an outbreak of spots? Well, if you do, drinking alcohol is just one way you can ruin the way your skin looks. This is because alcohol dehydrates your skin, sucking off all the moisture it needs, robbing your skin cells of their essential oxygen. This not only leads to dryness and blotchy skin but also causes premature ageing.

On top of this, alcohol takes vital nutrients like vitamins A and E away from your skin, and also contains tons of calories.

Long-term use of alcohol does something even nastier to your body. It causes blood vessels to dilate, increasing the risk of broken vessels around your face and causing a kind of permanent redness.

CHAPTER FOUR

Spots, acne and zits – what are they?

Think of all those names we have for spots. The nasty names we tease people with, the medical terms we classify spots with, and the descriptive words we torment ourselves with.

The fact is, spots are annoying, irritating and depressing. There's no getting away from it. However, they don't have to ruin your life if you take control of the situation.

In this chapter we tell you exactly what spots are, so that you're in the know and don't panic the next time one makes an appearance. Complete the quiz and find out how much you have already learnt about your skin.

The chances are you'll get spots at some stage during your life, so it's helpful to know exactly what they are so that you can take effective steps to get rid of them. There are an awful lot of myths surrounding spots, acne and zits – read on to find out the truth!

● QUIZ ●

WHAT'S WHAT WITH SPOTS?

1 What causes acne?
   a) Dirt
   b) Chocolate and chips
   c) Hormones

**2 Your sister and your mum have acne.
Will you get it too?**
   a) Not necessarily
   b) Yes
   c) No

3 Can make-up cause spots?
   a) Yes, it can block pores
   b) No, pores are blocked from the inside
   c) Not if you wear expensive make-up

4 Should you wash more if you have acne?
   a) Yes
   b) No
   c) Yes, and use a face scrub

5 Is acne infectious?
   a) Whiteheads and blackheads aren't,
      but pustules are
   b) No
   c) Yes

6 If you don't treat acne, will it eventually clear up on its own?
  a) Yes, but you have to wait until you're 18
  b) Yes, but it could take 20 years or more
  c) No

7 Is acne linked to sexual activity?
  a) Yes
  b) No
  c) Yes, it's something to do with using a sex hormone

8 If you have a healthy diet, exercise, never wear make-up and look after your skin, can you stay spot free?

a) Not a chance

b) Yes

c) Yes, but who wants to live like that

9 Boys get worse spots than girls because they...

a) Don't have to wear make-up

b) They don't, girls do because of periods

c) They have more of the sex hormone, testosterone

10 What percentage of people get spots?

a) 99.9%

b) 50%

c) 70%

ANSWERS

1	C	**2**	A	**3**	A
4	B	**5**	B	**6**	B
7	B	**8**	A	**9**	C
10	A				

How did you score? Under 3: you really, really need to read this chapter! 3–6: you did quite well, but you still need a few spot myths debunked. 7–10: you're doing well, but keep reading because there's still a lot you don't know.

WHAT IS A SPOT?

"They're those red lumpy things that get little yellow heads. They keep appearing all over your chin. Sometimes they're hard and sore and they might even look like insect bites, but they're not."

Rebecca, 14

"Spots look like bits of dirt stuck in your skin. Sometimes they can be white as well as black."

Tom, 13

A spot is all of the above and more. Sometimes it will be red, other times yellow, black or white. Spots tends to be fairly small and can appear anywhere on the face. Almost 99.9% of people get spots and pimples at some time in their life, while around 80% of teenagers get a condition called acne.

ARE SPOTS DIFFERENT TO ACNE?

 "Yes, I think that acne is something only boys get."

Jacqui, 12

 "Yes, acne is when your face is all red and you have hundreds of spots. You look like you've got the measles."

Harry, 12

Some dermatologists say spots are not the same as acne, because acne is a condition (i.e. more than one spot). However, the Acne Support Group say all spots are acne, simply because the same bacteria (priopionibacterium) is behind them all. Choose whatever name you want, because neither one is better than the other. If you feel comfortable with the term acne, then go for it; if not, spots is fine.

WHAT IS ACNE?

 "It's the germ that gives you a spot."

Tina, 14

 "Acne is the medical name for spots. That's what doctors call them."

Sue, 14

Acne is, in fact, the medical name given for spots (i.e. more than one, that frequently recur). Acne is a chronic condition triggered by male hormones known as androgens. These hormones control oil production in the skin of males and females. Usually the body's tiny oil producing sebaceous glands make enough lubrication (known as sebum) to keep the skin smooth and make hair shine. However, when these glands over-produce, as they do at puberty, the excess oil causes the hair follicle ducts to shed their lining too quickly, and dead skin cells begin to block up skin pores with sebum. Once plugged, the duct becomes blocked and can either cause the oil to solidify underneath (this is a blackhead or whitehead), or become inflamed when bacteria start to muscle in on the act. And this is what is known as a spot.

OW!

The spot will usually feel sore, and might throb slightly. If you press it, it will probably hurt and over time it will swell, until it ruptures.

WHY DOES ACNE OCCUR?

Acne develops because the sebaceous glands (the glands responsible for producing oil and lubricating the skin) become over-sensitive to testosterone in the body, and the glands go into over-production of oil. This means they produce too much sebum (the sticky substance which normally keeps the skin moist and supple).

When sebum is over-produced, it plugs up the gland outlet known as the skin pore, and mixes with bacteria on the skin's surface. When this happens the pore becomes inflamed with the sebum and bacteria, and begins to look angry (think red and swollen). This is because the spot has now become infected and filled with pus cells (a sure sign of infection). This is now known as a pustule – an inflamed spot of acne.

Inflamed spots: pustules, papules, nodules and cysts

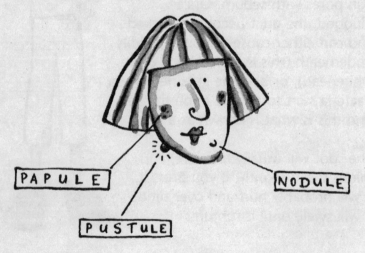

These look like red or yellow spots with centres. They can appear on or around the nose, on the chin, cheeks, back, chest area, and forehead.

Unlike whiteheads and blackheads, inflamed spots are known as pustules, papules, nodules or cysts. They are those nasty, red, painful spots that can cause you no end of bother. The reason they are so painful and long-lasting is because they involve a total blockage of the skin duct. This means all the oil and bacteria are swimming around together inside a swelling. Often these swellings start with a raised, red, hard lump that's a bit itchy and tender.

In severe cases, these lumps turn into nodules or cysts. These appear as large, tender, swollen lumps under the skin and are caused by scar tissue forming around an inflamed area. Never try to squeeze these nodules as you will make them rupture under the skin, causing the infection to spread.

If inflamed spots are left alone, they will eventually rupture and settle down on their own (though there are things you can do to help this process – see Chapter 5, page 70).

Non-inflamed spots: whiteheads or blackheads

Non-inflamed spots are called whiteheads or blackheads. These look like small black or white dots or raised areas of skin, which usually appear around the nose, forehead and chin.

According to the Acne Support Group, these occur when there is a blockage of the hair ducts due to an abnormality of the cells lining the duct. In normal skin, these cells continually grow and die and are shed on to the surface of the skin. In people with acne, the cells react to testosterone levels and become glue-like. This gloopy substance can't be shed, so it solidifies and blocks up the hair duct. The plug then becomes discoloured if it comes into contact with the air (a blackhead) or just pushes up the surface of the skin (a whitehead).

WHEN DOES ACNE OCCUR?

"Boys get spots when they become teenagers and start thinking about sex and things like that. Girls get acne when they start getting periods."

Steven, 13

Acne occurs more frequently at puberty simply because this is when teens become more sensitive to the high levels of hormones in their body. This means the body becomes flooded with testosterone (part of the androgen hormone group) and this directly leads to the development of spots and acne. Of course, this couldn't happen at a worse time because it's also at puberty that looks start to seem so important. However, it is important to realise that spots do not have to ruin your life. Instead of letting them take control of you, you should take control of them, and make a decision to not let them hold you back.

Acne really only occurs after puberty because this is when the sebaceous glands (where oil is produced) are over-stimulated by the sex hormone testosterone. Prior to puberty we have no sex hormones whizzing around our body and therefore nothing to affect our sebaceous glands. There are a few cases of juvenile acne which occur before puberty, but these are very rare.

WHERE WILL ACNE APPEAR?

"My sister says you can only get acne on your face, but I've heard you can get it anywhere, and that some people get it all over their body."

Dawn, 13

You'll be glad to hear that acne will not appear all over your body. It might, however, appear on your face, back and chest area. (Not everyone will get it on their back or chest area, some people may only find it on their faces.) More boys than girls find outbreaks in non-facial areas, simply because they have higher levels of testosterone in their bodies than girls.

ACNE: THE MYTHS – PART I

Chocolate causes spots or acne

This is probably the biggest spot myth. It's also a myth that chips and greasy food cause acne, though a well-balanced meal will help your skin to look healthier. Studies have shown over and over again that chocolate has nothing whatsoever to do with spots.

Toothpaste can zap a spot

Many people think fluoride in toothpaste can kill a spot. Unfortunately, this is not true and squeezing toothpaste on your spots is not that great for your skin, either – not to mention how silly you'll look if you go out with toothpaste all over your face.

The sun is good for spots

Not true. While the sun will zap acne, it's only a short-term effect. Long-term sun exposure will damage your skin in more ways than a spot ever will, by drying it out, causing premature ageing and increasing your risk of skin cancer.

Spots are caused by too much sex

Totally untrue. While spots are caused by the male sex hormone testosterone, having sex, not having sex, or even thinking about sex has no bearing on your skin. Testosterone is only called the sex hormone because it's the hormone responsible for our sexual development.

Acne's caused by dirt

Again, this is another myth. Many people think blackheads are bits of dirt, but they are really bits of sebum coloured by skin pigment which have turned dark because they have had contact with the air. Spots have nothing whatsoever to do with being unclean, or having dirt trapped in your skin.

Spots are contagious

This is complete rubbish. Spots are not at all contagious.

FACTORS WHICH CAN AFFECT ACNE

There are some factors besides hormones which can make your spots worse.

Periods

Surging levels of hormones around your period can cause spots, especially when levels of oestrogen and progestogen (the female hormones) drop out of sight just before your period. This gives the small amounts of testosterone in the female body the chance to wreak havoc on your skin.

Hot weather

Humid places (both foreign countries and close environments like steamy kitchens) cause spots in the same way that sweating does.

Make-up

Some cosmetics do cause acne, as do some suntan creams. This is because they are comedogenic which means they can help block an already partially blocked pore. If you have had a sudden acne flare-up, check whether or not your make-up brand is behind it by spot-testing an area of your face for 24 hours.

Ingredients in make-up that can aggravate acne:

- Mineral oil (like Vaseline) lies on the skin and is comedogenic, which means it blocks pores.
- Lanolin, found in lots of moisturising creams and suncreams is also comedogenic.

SPOTS AND ACNE: QUESTIONS AND ANSWERS

"Can I tell if I'm going to get acne when I reach puberty?"

Sam, 11

Acne is more common in people whose parents had acne, but it is not a definite sign you'll get spots. The fact is, there's no real way of predicting whether or not you'll be prone to acne. Even if your mum had the worse acne ever, there's no guarantee you'll follow in her footsteps.

"How come my mum still gets acne? She's thirty-five and she's still spotty."

Catherine, 12

Though many people associate acne with teenagers, the fact is that lots of people don't get it in their teens but do get it in their twenties and thirties. This is because acne is caused by an abnormal response to the hormone testosterone, which can happen at any age. However, it does tend to happen more commonly in teenagers, because it is then that hormone levels are more abnormal. As an adult, the reaction tends to be a sensitivity to normal levels of testosterone. Acne in adults is treated the same way as it is treated in teenagers.

"Please tell me once and for all, do chocolate and chips cause spots? I've heard they do, but some of my friends (who aren't spotty like me) eat them and they don't have spots."

Lisa, 14

Happily for most people, research now shows that spots aren't caused by chocolate, sweets and or chips. Parents usually spin this one as a way of getting you to cut back on junk food.

"You say chocolates don't cause spots, but whenever I eat chocolate I get spots."

Chloe, 13

Some girls do find there is a link between their spots and how much chocolate they eat. If this is the case for you, look closely at your chocolate eating habits. Do you eat more chocolate at certain times of the month – like when you are pre-menstrual (the week before your period)? Is this the time you also get spots? If so, it's not the chocolate causing the spots, but your hormone levels which fluctuate prior to your period. If you are still not convinced, try excluding chocolate from your diet for at least six weeks and you'll see it has no effect.

> *"I wash my face all the time and yet I still have spots. What am I doing wrong?"*
>
> Tom, 14

Nothing. Spots have nothing to do with how clean you are. The infection which causes a spot starts from the inside of your skin, not the outside, so no amount of washing will help you to avoid spots. But keeping surface dirt away will give your skin a better chance of avoiding blocked pores.

> *"I have been told I have acne on my face, but now I have similar spots on my back and chest. Am I allergic to something?"*
>
> Anne, 15

Don't worry: acne is not an allergy. Acne often occurs on your back and chest as well as your face. This is because the sebaceous (oil) glands also occur on the back and chest. If you have acne in these areas, treat it the way you would treat the spots on your face. For starters, wear breathable clothes like cotton, so sweat can be absorbed more easily and not just lie over the skin. Even spots on the back can scar if you don't get them treated.

"What is Acne Rosacea?"

Dawn, 14

Acne Rosacea is also known as adult acne because it primarily affects adults. Unlike ordinary acne, Acne Rosacea is an inflammatory skin disorder that is thought to be fungal in origin. It hits the central part of the face, making the whole cheek and nose area very red, accompanied in some cases by pustules (hence the acne association). This condition usually affects more men than women and occurs anywhere between the ages of 30 and 50 years. Treatment is with antibiotics through your GP.

CHAPTER FIVE

Conquering acne

THE PSYCHOLOGICAL IMPACT OF ACNE

"The worse thing about spots is boys don't fancy you. They think you're ugly because your face is all ruined."

Sara, 12

"Girls don't fancy me because of my face. It's like one big spot."

Harry, 12

"I don't do a lot of things because of the way I look. I know it's stupid but I hate the way I look, so I know other people will too. My mum says I should not put my head down so much but I can't help it."

Sharma, 12

"I get picked on quite a bit at school. My mates think it's funny to call me names because I have spots. They don't realise how hurt it makes me feel."

Lisa 13

If you've ever had acne, you'll know that the big problem with it isn't the actual spots, but the living with it; having to look in a mirror and see it apparently grow and take over your face. The idea that everyone else can see it, and that somehow you imagine it's all your fault. What's worse is the knowledge that you have to wait to grow out of it.

Well, we're here to tell you don't have to wait. You can do something about your acne and you can help yourself right now. Just read this chapter and take our advice.

ACNE: THE MYTHS - PART 2

Myth no. 1: DON'T PICK YOUR SPOTS

"My mum goes mad when I pick my spots. She says I am making them worse. But sometimes I just can't help it."

Helen, 14

How many times have you heard the following?

"Don't pick your spots because you'll get scars."
"Don't pick your spots because you'll spread the infection."
"Don't pick your spots because you'll make them look worse."
"Don't pick your spots because it's not hygienic."

Well, in an ideal world you shouldn't pick your spots because all of the above are true.

However, everyone picks their spots, partly because it's so tempting to, but also because most people are eager to get rid of their pustules and pimples. So, if you want to squeeze your spots, do it properly and follow the Acne Support Group's Guide to Sensible Squeezing.

Think traffic lights. If your spots are…

RED: Stop! Sorry, you can't squeeze this one. This is a 'blind' type of spot (a papule) which is lurking beneath the skin's surface. This means no amount of squeezing will get it out. If you try to squeeze it, you may cause the infection to sink deeper into the skin and the spot will last twice as long.

YELLOW: Ready! This is a pustule – a spot ripe to be picked (see below for squeezing guide), as it has come to the surface of your skin and is about to rupture.

GREEN: Don't worry, spots don't go green!

The Guide to Sensible Squeezing

1 Wash your hands with soap. Spots are caused by bacteria and your hands carry heaps of them, so if you're going to touch your face, make sure your hands and nails are clean and there are no bugs on your mitts.

2 Don't squeeze with your fingernails unless you'd like a nice nail imprint on your skin, which will draw lots more attention to your spots. Always be gentle with your skin. Use two tissues and the sides of your fingers when attempting to draw out a spot.

3 Don't squeeze inwards, but pull the skin apart between the sides of your fingers, away from the centre of the spot. If a zit is ready to pop, this will work and cause less trauma to the skin. If this doesn't work, then gently squeeze with both fingers, pushing the spot inwards. This creates pressure which should be enough to pop the spot. You should not squeeze till clear liquid comes out or the spot bleeds. Also, remember that you are aiming to release the contents of the spot, not perform a miracle. Popping a spot will never make it immediately disappear. Your skin will be left sore and a little swollen.

4 Do not immediately apply make-up or astringent. Give your freshly squeezed spot at least an hour to dry up and then try dabbing tea tree oil (a natural oil with anti-bacterial properties) on to it.

Myth no. 2: IGNORE YOUR SPOTS

"My dad says I should ignore my spots as I'll grow out of them sooner or later. I really hate having such bad spots, but my dad says I ought to just leave them alone."

Tim, 14

Most people are lucky enough to grow out of their spots. However, you don't have to wait to grow out of them or ignore them (which is pretty impossible anyway). There are a number of things you can do and places you can go for help.

For a start, you can try an over-the-counter product like the ones recommended on pages 74 and 75, see your GP or visit a dermatologist (skin specialist).

You can also learn all you need to know about acne so you'll be able to make the right choices for yourself and decide what you want to do. Learning about acne will also help you to realise that your spots aren't your fault, or the result of anything you did. You can call the Acne Support Group whose details are listed on page 92, or go to their website and look up acne.

Finally, you can cover spots up, especially if you're going somewhere special or on a date. Of course, it's not a good idea to smother them in make-up or hide them under your hair. But let's be realistic here: one night of covering them up isn't going to ruin your skin. Just make sure you take the make-up off later and clean your face properly.

Myth no. 3: NATURAL IS BEST

"My sister says I should give natural products a try because they have been proven to be really good for the skin. I'm not so sure. Some of them sound pretty iffy to me."

Tom, 14

There's been a lot written about natural products and their 'miracle' anti-acne properties. In some cases, natural products do work. However, there have been no clinical studies that prove any natural product works wonders on acne. So, if you want to give a natural product a try, go ahead. Apply the two month rule to it (see below) and don't pay a fortune for anything. If it works for you, great; if it doesn't, it's time to take other action. Remember, tea tree oil is one of the few natural products that have been proven to help.

Natural products said to work against acne:

- **Spirulina:** a form of blue/green algae either swallowed in pill form or used as a mask. Said to work against spots because it contains all eight essential amino acids. Available from health food shops.
- **Zinc:** supplements of 30 mg a day are said to work against acne in the same way as some antibiotics.
- **Flaxseed oil:** a fatty acid which helps create anti-inflammatory substances in the body.
- **Tea tree and lavender oils:** highly antiseptic and can be applied topically (i.e. right on top of your spots).
- **Acupuncture:** this can decrease inflammation.

- **Forsythia and honeysuckle pod:** natural antibiotics with anti-inflammatory properties.

TOUGHER ACTION AGAINST SPOTS

Self medication

"I've heard miracle spots cures don't work and are a waste of money. Is that true? There are loads of spot cures in the shops. Surely some of them should be able to help?"

Jenny, 12

While miracle overnight cures don't work, a number of over-the-counter products (i.e. products which you buy from chemists) can help if you give them time. The Acne Support Group suggest applying the two month rule to any acne treatment you try. This means that if you do not see a 35% to 50% marked improvement in your skin after eight weeks of using the product (i.e. going from 10 spots down to 5 or 6 spots), new action should be taken.

People with low to moderate acne could try a product containing Benzoyl Peroxide (available from the chemist). This is a powerful oxidising agent and on the skin it acts as a peeling and anti-blackhead agent. Regular use is supposed to loosen blackheads and allow them to be shed. This product also has germicidal activity and therefore reduces the amount of bacteria on the skin. Make sure you always start with a low dosage (2.5% of this ingredient) and then work up to a larger strength if necessary. This is because a high dose can burn the skin and make it turn red. Benzoyl Peroxide can irritate the skin, though the skin tolerates it more as time progresses.

If this has no effect, try a product with the active ingredient Azelaic acid (also available from the chemist). This is a substance which can kill bacteria and unblock plugged-up hair follicles by loosening blackheads. Again, give it two months and increase the dosage gradually if necessary.

Seeing your doctor

No decent doctor worth their salt will laugh at you or turn you away if you go to see them about acne. If they do, it's time to change doctors. Most now know that acne and spots are a serious condition that affects their patients' lives dramatically. So if you want to take tougher action against your spots, make an appointment today – you won't be sorry.

Of course, it can be pretty scary having to talk to a doctor about your skin. But there are a number of ways you can help yourself.

- Be informed. If you don't know what kind of help is available, ask questions and keep asking until you understand.
- Take someone along for support (e.g. your mum).
- Read up on what to ask for before you see your doctor (The Acne Support Group can help you here).
- If a doctor won't help you, ask to see someone else.
- Don't let the doctor fob you off with the 'you'll grow out of it' line. You want help and you're entitled to it.

Possible dialogue you could have with your doctor:

The doctor says: *"You'll grow out of it."*
You say: *"Yes, but I don't want to wait that long. I need help now before I get scarring."*

The doctor says: *"They're only spots!"*
You say: *"Yes, but they are affecting my life. They make me feel depressed"* *(or miserable, unconfident, etc.).*

| The doctor says: | "I only treat serious conditions." |
| You say: | "This feels serious to me because it's affecting my life." |

| The doctor says: | "Take these, they'll cure it." |
| You say: | "What are they and how will they work? Also, how long do I have to take them for? Will they have any side effects?" |

Antibiotics

There are many antibiotic treatments available from your GP which can help fight acne. The main ones are tetracycline, doxycycline, minocycline and erythromycin. Be aware that they can take up to six months to work, so you need to persevere and not give up.

Topical antibiotics are antibiotics which are applied to your skin in a lotion form. They work by being absorbed into the skin where they reduce the level of bacteria and inflammation. They are usually prescribed for people who have mild to moderate acne with pustules. They need to be used twice a day, regardless of whether a spot is present or not.

Oral antibiotics are antibiotics which you swallow in a pill form. They are usually prescribed for six months and work by reducing levels of bacteria in the skin and reducing inflammation.

Tetracyclines are the most frequently prescribed antibiotic for acne. The big disadvantage with tetracycline is that it is not absorbed properly if you eat something with it, so it needs to be taken with water on an empty stomach, half an hour before you eat. Milk will also make it ineffective, so no tea or milkshakes half an hour before or after you take it.

A full course of antibiotics need to be taken before you can decide if they have worked for you or not. If after six months your acne has not improved by at least 50%, then you need to go back to your GP and asked to be referred to a dermatologist.

The big side-effect of antibiotics for girls is that they can interfere with the contraceptive pill and may make it unsafe.

The Pill

There is one type of contraceptive pill which can help zap acne. It is known as Dianette® and is available from your GP. That aside, if you intend to go on a contraceptive pill, it's always worth discussing any acne concerns with your GP first, as some contraceptive pills can aggravate acne.

Dermatologists and Roaccutane (Isotretinoin)

Roaccutane has been available in the UK for about fifteen years and in the United States for twenty. This drug can only be prescribed by a hospital dermatologist (you need to be referred by your GP) and is only used on patients who have severe acne, who have tried several courses of antibiotics without success, or whose acne is causing bad scarring.

All patients on Roaccutane are closely watched because of several side effects, which can include dry skin, depression, eczema, headaches, facial redness and muscle and joint pain. That aside, Roaccutane has revolutionised the treatment of severe acne as it is the only drug which works on most aspects of acne: it helps to dry up excess oil, stop sebum production, reduce inflammation and lessens subsequent scarring. About seventy-five per cent of people who take this drug do not have a relapse.

Generally, results can be seen within a couple of weeks after starting treatment, though it is usual to have a flare up, up to six weeks into the course. Most people find their acne clears up totally after a four-month course.

SCARRING

"My brother's spots have left lots of marks on his face. How can I make sure this doesn't happen to me?"
Gemma, 12

Scar tissue, whatever it's caused by, will never go back to 'perfect' skin. All you can do is hope to improve the condition by seeking help for your acne. Remember, scarring is a permanent reminder of a temporary problem. There are two types of scars associated with acne: pitted scarring and keloid scars.

Pitted scars look like small pits or dents in the skin, very much like chicken pox scars. These scars are caused by a loss of collagen, the tissue in the skin that plumps it up. It happens when pus and inflammation inside a spot damage the structure of the skin. The body tries to heal this damage (like it does with cuts and abrasions) with scar tissue. This scar tissue eventually becomes the pit and once the scar has formed it is permanent, though it will probably fade with time.

Keloid scars are raised, lumpy scars. They occur because they are part of an abnormal healing process where the body produces too much scar tissue. While they can occur on the face, these type of scars usually appear on the back and chest. You can identify them by a slight itchiness, smooth surface and round or oblong shape. Your doctor can treat keloid scars, making them flatter and less itchy, but they will still mark the skin to some degree.

The tough thing about scarring is that it's hard to eliminate. There are a number of laser and surgery techniques that can reduce the effects of scars. But most of these are not available on the NHS and cost between £350 to £3000. For the ones available on the NHS, waiting lists are in excess of a year, and you cannot go on the list until you are eighteen years old. So try to avoid the hassle of treating scars by taking early action with your spots.

Dermabrasion

This is a technique whereby the top layer of scarred skin is buffed away from the face. It leaves the skin very sore and sensitive to sunlight for a number of weeks. Thankfully it is used less often these days, as lasers are the usual first choice.

THE DOCTOR IS IN

Laser treatment

This is a cosmetic process which has replaced dermabrasion and works as a re-surfacing technique. This means a laser is used to vaporise the outer layers of the skin, leaving finer skin on the surface. When this skin heals, surface wrinkles and small scars may be obliterated.

Collagen injections

This is a process where collagen is injected into scars to even them out. The results, unfortunately, are not permanent and cost up to £500 a time.

SELF-HELP TIPS FOR YOUR SKIN

- Many skin treatments dry out the skin, so make sure you use an oil free moisturiser (cream or lotion) on your face.
- If you wear make-up remember to use non-oily brands.
- Make sure suncream is non-oily too.
- Apply acne medication on all affected areas, not just on spots.
- If you have any kind of allergic reaction, stop taking the treatment right away, although a degree of redness or even flakiness is often to be expected with some treatments.
- Always wash your hands before you touch your face to stop you spreading more bacteria.
- Remember, acne will eventually clear up. You won't have it for ever.

● CHAPTER SIX ●

The practical guide to living with spots

FIGHTING THE SPOT POLICE

"Everyone is always giving me advice about my spots.
Advice I don't even ask for. My aunts come round and
suggest that maybe I eat too much fat, or wear the
wrong make-up. My parents are always telling me it's
because my hair is over my face. Even my PE teacher
suggests it's because I don't do enough exercise. I get
really sick of it. I know I have spots, I know they look
horrible, I don't need to be reminded about it all the time."

Laurie, 14

By this stage of the book you should know exactly
what spots are, why you get them, and what you
can do to zap them. All that's left to learn is how to
live with them. Not the easiest thing the world, when
everyone, especially adults, act like the spot police.
However, before you write this chapter off as a
happy-clappy-wear-your-spots-with-pride chapter, let
me reassure you that learning to live with your spots

doesn't mean learning to like them. We all know that pretending your spots aren't bothering you, when they are, is no practical solution. Thankfully, there are plenty of things you can do which will not only help you deal with the actual spots, but also with the zillions of people who pass comments on them.

If you don't want the spot police to ruin your life, try any of the following bits of dialogue.

They say: "You shouldn't cover your spots up with make-up."

You say: "Actually, dermatologists say it's fine, as long as I wash the make-up off properly afterwards."

They say "You shouldn't cover your spots with hair."

You say: "Why not? Hair touching skin has nothing to do with spots, especially if the hair is clean."

They say "Have you tried…"

You say: "No, I'm treating my spots with my doctor's help."

They say "You get spots because you eat the wrong things…"

You say: "Actually, spots aren't caused by food. They're caused by overactive oil glands blocking the pores."

They say "Don't bother worrying. You'll grow out of it."

You say: "Why wait? I can treat them now."

PARENTS AND SPOTS

"My parents are always going on at me about my spots. Like it's my fault I've got them. My dad is the worst. He's always saying, 'Look at your skin! What a mess. Stop picking at them. Leave them alone.' He just doesn't understand how I feel at all."

Tim, 14

"My mum says I have spots because I eat the wrong things. The minute I eat chocolate or a biscuit, she tuts at me and says it will give me spots. I feel bad enough already without her watching me all the time."

Alison, 13

"My mum says the best cure for spots is witch-hazel. She won't buy me anything but this and when my spots get worse, she just says I haven't been using it properly. I want to try something else, but I don't have the money."

Suzanne, 12

"My dad says my spots are caused by wearing too much make-up and staying up late. Because of this he has banned me from staying up later than 10 p.m. and won't let me buy make-up."

Sian, 13

The trouble with spots and parents is that nearly all parents have a strong opinion about spots and what causes them. They also think they know how to treat them, simply because they once had them too. On a positive note, this means your parents should be more sympathetic about what you're going through; but on a negative note, this also means they're going to have a whole host of spot myths to pass on to you. Myths you're going to have to sift through and deal with before you start getting to grips with your acne.

According to surveys, 83% of young people seek advice from their parents about spots. The problem is, the majority of parents aren't as knowledgeable about spots as they think. This is mainly because views on spots have changed over the years, as have the medications available. For example, once it was widely believed that diet played a major role in the development of acne, and now we know better thanks to new scientific evidence. This is why it's important to become informed about spots, so that you know exactly what you should and should not be doing for them. So your first step has to be to sift through what your parents tell you.

They say:	*"It's your fault you're getting spots; you eat too much junk."*
They might mean:	*"I don't want you to eat so much junk and so I'm going to scare you off it."*
Your response might be:	*to eat more junk food as a retaliation.*

Instead, why not: acknowledge that while junk doesn't cause acne, good food does help create healthy skin. Compromise by cutting down on your junk, but still treat yourself occasionally.

They say: "Try using this. It worked for me."

They might mean: "I want to help."

Your response might be: "No way."

Instead, why not: try the product and if it has no effect, tell your parents about your medical options and suggest one of them comes with you to the doctor.

Just leave me alone!

They say:	"You're not washing your face properly."
They might mean:	"I want to help you but I don't know how."
Your response might be:	Anger.
Instead, why not:	explain that over-washing hinders spots not helps them, and ask what they think about you seeking help from an expert.

They say:	"Look at your face – stop picking your spots."
They might mean:	"You're going to scar yourself for life and I don't want you to do that to yourself."
Your response might be:	to feel upset because they don't understand how you feel.
Instead, why not:	tell them how having spots makes you feel. Explain that picking is your way of trying to get rid of the spots.

They say:	"You'll never get a boyfriend/girlfriend if you don't do something about your spots."
They might mean:	"I think your spots are to do with something you're doing wrong and I want to stop you doing it."

Your response might be: to feel angry and upset with them and yourself.

Instead, why not: ask them to be supportive in helping you deal with your spots, as they are making you feel bad about yourself.

Remember:

* Your parents do want to help you. They just don't know how.
* Your parents don't know everything when it comes to spots.
* Your parents also had spots, so if you explain your feelings to them, they will understand.
* Your parents may try to use your spots as an excuse to make you change certain habits.
* Your parents can't help commenting on your spots, because they often forget you are a rational person with feelings and opinions.
* They won't know you're bothered about your spots unless you tell them.
* If your parents are short of cash and can't afford to get you some of the over-the-counter products, do go and see your GP as you can get free medication on prescription.

So finally, here is a checklist of fifteen top tips for healthy skin.

1   Try not to pick your spots because this can lead to scarring. You can't treat scars completely, but you *can* treat spots.

2 If you are unhappy with your skin, *seek help*. Try different medications (remember to use the two month rule recommended by the Acne Support Group) and if they don't work, go and see your doctor.

3 Try to get at least eight hours sleep to help your skin renew itself.

4 Don't smoke, drink alcohol or take drugs as this will damage your skin.

5 Do some exercise to improve your circulation.

6 Cleanse your face twice a day to help prevent pores from becoming blocked.

7 Don't scrub your skin as this will damage it.

8 Don't over-wash your skin: be gentle with it.

9 Girls, take your make-up off at night.

10 Boys, learn to shave properly.

11 Wear a moisturiser with SPF 15.

12 Drink lots of water and eat a balanced diet with plenty of fresh fruit and vegetables.

13 Don't waste your money on 'miracle' products.

14 Try to wear cotton clothing which allows your skin to breathe.

15 Remember, stress can lead to spots, so try to relax and stay cool.

Good luck with your skin!

Useful telephone numbers

If you need further information or advice about the issues covered in this book, contact one of the organisations listed below.

Acne Support Group – 020 8841 4747

You can send an SAE for a free acne factsheet to: The Acne Support Group, Howard House, The Runway, Ruislip, Middlesex, HA4 6FE.

ASH (freefone helpline for advice on giving up smoking) 0800 002200

Childline (freefone confidential helpline) 0800 1111

The Sports Council – 020 7388 1277

The Health Education Authority (HEA) publish leaflets and books on a range of health topics, which are usually available at a local health promotion clinic (check in the phone book for your nearest clinic).

Glossary

ACNE
the medical name given to spots.

ACNE ROSACEA
also known as adult acne because it primarily affects adults.
Unlike ordinary acne, Acne Rosacea is an inflammatory skin
disorder that is thought to be fungal, not bacterial in origin.

BENZOYL PEROXIDE
a powerful oxidising agent. When used on the skin it acts as a
peeling and anti-blackhead agent.

BLACKHEADS/WHITEHEADS
Non-inflamed spots. Small black or white dots or raised areas of
skin, which usually appear around the nose, forehead and chin.

COLLAGEN
a connective substance in the skin tissue.

COMBINATION SKIN
dry, flaky cheeks, and an oily T-zone, going from your forehead
down your nose to your chin.

DERMATOLOGIST
skin doctor.

DRY SKIN
skin which tends to looks red in patches and be flaky.
Sometimes the skin will looked chapped and peeling.

MALIGNANT MELANOMA
cancer of the pigment cells of the skin.

OILY SKIN
skin which is shiny, even when it's not hot. With large pores.

PUSTULES, PAPULES, NODULES AND CYSTS
all types of inflamed spots of acne.

SEBACEOUS GLANDS
the glands responsible for producing oil and lubricating the skin.

SEBUM
the sticky lubricating substance which normally keeps the skin moist and supple, produced by the body's tiny oil sebaceous glands.

SENSITIVE SKIN
skin which is blotchy, sometimes itchy and reacts quickly to certain types of cosmetics and soaps and sometimes to extremes in temperature.

SKIN
your body's largest living, breathing organ. The super strong, protective, outer layer between your vital organs and the world of germs, bacteria and pollution.

SKIN PORE
also known as the gland outlet and/or duct.

SPOT
a bacteria-based blemish on the skin's surface (see Acne).

Index

h HODDER

Another Hodder Children's book

BULLYING

Michele Elliott

Nearly everyone is bullied at some point in their life. But what exactly does bullying mean? Are there practical things you can do to stop it? How do you deal with your anger and frustration? How can you learn to make friends and respect yourself? If you're a bully, can you ever change your behaviour?

Don't suffer in silence. Learn how to beat the bullies and restore your self-esteem with this essential wise guide.

Another Hodder Children's book

DIVORCE & SEPARATION

Matthew Whyman

Are your mum and dad splitting up?
What does a divorce actually involve?
How can you cope with your feelings?
What happens if a parent meets
someone new?
What is it like living with a stepfamily?

This essential wise guide gives you
down-to-earth and reassuring advice to
help you through your parents' divorce.

Another Hodder Children's book

DRUGS

Anita Naik

What are drugs?
What do they do to your mind –
and your body?
Are you under pressure to take drugs?
Do you have friends who already do?
What are the risks – and how should
you deal with them?

Alcohol and amphetamines, tobacco and
cannabis, solvents and steroids – know
the realities and explode the myths with
this essential wise guide.

Another Hodder Children's book

EATING

Anita Naik

Do you worry about your weight?
Do you wish you looked like a supermodel?
Are you always on a diet?
Does eating make you feel guilty?

From crash diets and calorie-counting to
anorexia and bulimia – find out the facts
about food and you, and learn to love your
body with this essential wise guide.

Another Hodder Children's book

PERIODS

Charlotte Owen

Everyone worries about getting their
first period.
What does it mean?
When will it happen?
How will it feel?
Will everyone else know?
And what on earth do you do?

This essential book explains all you'll
ever need to know about one of the most
important times in your life!

SELF ESTEEM

Anita Naik

Are you scared to take risks in case you
make a fool of yourself?
Do you need other people's approval?
If a boy likes you, do you think there
must be something wrong with him?
Do you hate your body?

If you answered yes to any of these
questions, you need to improve your
self esteem! Learn to believe in yourself
and get ready for a positive future with this
essential wise guide.

Another Hodder Children's book

SEX

Anita Naik

What do you know about sex?
How will you know when you're ready?
Can you trust your emotions?
Can you resist the pressure and say no?
Would you know how to protect yourself
if you said yes?

Periods and puberty, crushes and
contraception, health and harassment –
know the realities and explode the myths
with this essential wise guide.

SMOKING

Matthew Whyman

Are you tempted to start smoking?
Do you want to know the damage to your
health and wallet?
Are you tired of choking on other
people's smoke?
Maybe you need to help to stub out
the habit?

Whether you want to avoid the temptation
to light up or you're desperate to quit –
this essential wise guide explodes
the myths and gives you all the facts so
you can make your own decisions.

Another Hodder Children's book

YOUR RIGHTS

Anita Naik

If you take something back to a shop,
do they have to give you a refund?
If your parents get divorced, can you decide
who you live with?
Can you have a job however old you are?
Can a teacher hit you?
What would actually happen if you were
caught drinking under age?

If you've ever wondered what you are
allowed to do in all sorts of everyday
situations, and how the law affects you,
find out your rights in this essential
wise guide.

ORDER FORM
Wise Guides

0 340 71483 2	BULLYING	£3.99
0 340 75297 1	DIVORCE & SEPARATION	£3.99
0 340 69973 6	DRUGS	£3.99
0 340 74411 1	EATING	£3.99
0 340 63604 1	PERIODS	£3.99
0 340 75299 8	SELF-ESTEEM	£3.99
0 340 71042 X	SEX	£3.99
0 340 77842 3	SMOKING	£3.99
0 340 74419 7	YOUR RIGHTS	£3.99

All Hodder Children's books are available at your local bookshop or newsagent, or can be ordered direct from the publisher. Just tick the titles you want and fill in the form below. Prices and availability subject to change without notice.

Hodder Children's Books, Cash Sales Department, Bookpoint, 39 Milton Park, Abingdon, Oxon, OX14 4TD, UK. If you have a credit card you may order by telephone – (01235) 400414. Please enclose a cheque or postal order made payable to Bookpoint Ltd to the value of the cover price and allow the following for postage and packing:

UK & BFPO – £1.00 for the first book, 50p for the second book, and 30p for each additional book ordered, up to a maximum charge of £3.00.

OVERSEAS & EIRE – £2.00 for the first book, £1.00 for the second book, and 50p for each additional book.

Name ....

Address ....

....

....

If you would prefer to pay by credit card, please complete the following: Please debit my Visa/Access/Diner's Card/American Express (delete as applicable) card no:

----- ----- ----- ----- ----- ----- ----- ----- ----- ----- ----- ----- ----- ----- ----- -----

Signature ....

Expiry Date ....